Farang

ฝรั่ง

Farang

poems by
Peter Blair

Autumn House Press
Pittsburgh

AN ESTHER HARDER BOOK

For permission to reprint any part of this book contact:
Autumn House Press
87 1/2 Westwood Street
Pittsburgh, PA 15211.
Telephone: 412-381-4261.
Website: www.autumnhouse.org.

Autumn House and Autumn House Press are registered trademarks owned by Autumn House Press, a 501c3 (non-profit) corporation with the mission of publishing poetry and other fine literature.

Autumn House Press Staff
Editor-in-Chief and Poetry Editor: Michael Simms
Executive Director: Richard St. John
Co-Founder: Eva-Maria Simms
Fiction Editor: Sharon Dilworth
Coal Hill Founder and Technical Editor: Joshua Storey
Community Outreach Director: Michael Wurster
Associate Editor: Esther Harder
Assistant Editor: Evan Oare
Media Consultant: Jan Beatty
Publishing Consultant: Peter Oresick
Editorial Consultant: Ziggy Edwards
Tech Crew Chief: Michael Milberger
Intern: Christina Haaf

This project was supported by The Pennsylvania Council on the Arts, a state agency, through its regional arts funding partnership, Pennsylvania Partners in the Arts (PPA). State government funding comes through an annual appropriation by Pennsylvania's General Assembly. PPA is administered in Allegheny County by Greater Pittsburgh Arts Council.

Library of Congress number: 2009933535
ISBN: 978-1-932870-34-3

Acknowledgements:

These journals have published the following poems:

Buffalo Bones:
  "Making Sticky Rice on Edgerton Place"
Natural Bridge:
  "The Day after the Coup"
Pigeon Creek:
  "With Yingna at the Hotel Opera Coffee Shop"
  "Traffic Circle"
The Pittsburgh Quarterly Online:
  "November Full Moon"
poetrymagazine.com:
  "Farang"
Visions International:
  "Discussing the Dream of Culture with Professor Kwaam"
The Writer's Quill:
  "Planting Rice with Nipun, Ubol Province"
  and a section of "Like a Stone under Water"

"Up-country" won Honorable Mention in the Billee Murray Denny Poetry Contest, and was published in the anthology, *The Denny Poems*.

Any similarity to persons living or dead in this book is purely coincidental. The folktale in "The Night House" is adapted from *Little Things*, by Prajuab Thirabutana.

I'd like to thank the following people for their help, and/or careful reading of some or all of the manuscript: Marcelle Crickenberger, Pamela Richardson, Greg Wickliff, Ed Geibel, Ed Moore. I also want to thank Elizabeth Gargano who read every poem and gave helpful suggestions every step of the way, and whose insight and care for language are extraordinary.

I'd like to thank Michael Simms for his suggestions and editorial work, and the fact that this project started with his notice of a single poem of mine which then grew over the years into this book.

The Autumn House Poetry Series

Michael Simms, Editor-in-Chief

Snow White Horses, Selected Poems 1973-88
by Ed Ochester

The Leaving, New and Selected Poems
by Sue Ellen Thompson

Dirt by Jo McDougall

Fire in the Orchard by Gary Margolis

Just Once, New and Previous Poems
by Samuel Hazo

*The White Calf Kicks
by Deborah Slicer, 2003,
selected by Naomi Shihab Nye

The Divine Salt by Peter Blair

The Dark Takes Aim by Julie Suk

Satisfied with Havoc by Jo McDougall

Half Lives by Richard Jackson

Not God After All by Gerald Stern
(with drawings by Sheba Sharrow)

*Dear Good Naked Morning
by Ruth L. Schwartz, 2004,
selected by Alicia Ostriker

A Flight to Elsewhere by Samuel Hazo

Collected Poems by Patricia Dobler

*The Autumn House Anthology of
Contemporary American Poetry*, edited by
Sue Ellen Thompson

Déjà Vu Diner by Leonard Gontarek

*lucky wreck by Ada Limon, 2005, selected
by Jean Valentine

The Golden Hour
by Sue Ellen Thompson

Woman in the Painting
by Andrea Hollander Budy

*Joyful Noise: An Anthology of American
Spiritual Poetry,*
edited by Robert Strong

*No Sweeter Fat by Nancy Pagh, 2006,
selected by Tim Seibles

Unreconstructed: Poems Selected and New
by Ed Ochester

Rabbis of the Air by Philip Terman

*Let it be a Dark Roux: New and Selected
Poems* by Sheryl St. Germain

Dixmont by Rick Campbell

The River is Rising
by Patricia Jabbeh Wesley

*The Dark Opens by Miriam Levine, 2007,
selected by Mark Doty

The Song of the Horse by Samuel Hazo

My Life as a Doll
by Elizabeth Kirschner

She Heads into the Wilderness
by Anne Marie Macari

*When She Named Fire, An Anthology of
Contemporary Poetry by American Women,*
edited by Andrea Hollander Budy

*A Theory of Everything
by Mary Crockett Hill, 2008,
selected by Naomi Shihab Nye

*What the Heart can Bear: Selected and
Uncollected Poems 1979-1993*
by Robert Gibb

Blood Honey by Chana Bloch

Farang by Peter Blair

*Winners of the annual Autumn House Poetry Prize

for Beth

Contents

IV. The Land of Transit

Insight means diving into the deep water of sensation.

Bikkhu Nagasena

November Full Moon

Discussing the Dream of Culture
with Professor Kwaam

At the corner of Somprasong and Petchaburi
we sit at a rickety metal table. Our soup steams
in sidewalk sunlight. Cars crawl on the street
like the streams of ants up and down the shop wall.
His shiny head fuzzed with new hair,
eyebrows shaved clean, Kwaam smiles, ethereal,
kind: *Thai and American cultures, two dreams
of one world, the Dharma.* A few months ago
he taught me Thai and how to read palms:
A good way to hold hands with a girl. He winked.
Now, he's one day out of a monastery and saffron
robes. Noodles slip off my novice chopsticks.
My soup darkened by soy sauce, peanuts,
sugar, the strands disappear in my bowl.
Kwaam's noodles twine in clear broth.

At the plywood counter, I buy another soup.
The cook dunks a strainer of beef chunks
in boiling water. The red meat turns gray
and rubbery in bubbling froth. He dumps them
into a bowl with cilantro, sprouts, broth
and a fleshy lump of noodles. *So, what is Dharma?*
I set the dish on the table. *Dharma is the empty
bowl.* Joking, again. The sky's blue, like a bowl
overturned on market stalls and bleached
white buildings. *The abbot took us to an autopsy.
They cut open a woman, removed the heart,
liver, intestines.* He tells me about shriveled skin,
hollow rib cages arching over tables,
pails of limp, gray organs. *Dharma.*

My soup steams. My abdomen's distended.
The market gurgles ageless sounds around us.
I can't look at Kwaam's sad, triumphant smile,
or the emptiness deepening in his sunlit bowl.

Farang

Night in the Mississippi Queen
on Patpong Road, Phanni's hands
rub my back, silky snakes
up and down my spine.
Swaying on platforms,
bikini-girls dance, hypnotic
in swirls of cigarette smoke
and incense. In the mirror's glitter,
I watch Phanni's oval sienna face
eclipsed by naked legs,
whisper in my ear: *I do*
anything for you. Try me.

Let's go till dawn,
Harry says, walking, 4 a.m.
In a market, sellers part the flaps
of their mosquito nets, yawn
and stretch. Bloody eyes
follow us from a stall.
A buffalo's skull leers
from behind the red mound
of its butchered flesh.

Ghost-like, saffron shadows
stir the morning fog. Monks
pause by a woman kneeling.
She bows low, her nose to the toes
of the monks' sandaled feet,
extends her arm above her head,
drops banana-leaf rice packets
into the black globes of their bowls.

A sucking *woof,* like a snuffed
candle flame against
my ear, the stone just misses,
clatters into the closed metal
shop gates. *Farang! Foreigner!*
floats in from wherever
my fear is. Across the street,
six trishaw drivers lounge,
feet up on handlebars, smiling.

Siripan's Father

The night we stay late in the closed library,
she tells me her father doesn't like her
dating a *farang.* She undoes her black hair,
lets it hang to the chair seat, a dark curtain.

At 80, he still sprints each morning, bony legs
pumping under ragged shorts, wind blowing
the silver curls of his whiskers. A GI on the street
once yelled out: *Number 1 mustache,*
and he never shaved it again. His bare feet
swish the dirt road as if he were still escaping
the Red Chinese. At 14, he left his parents
on Hainan Island, walked through starved villages
where the bark had been eaten off trees,
sailed steerage south to Thailand.
In Bangkok, he opened a market stall,
met a dark Thai girl carrying baskets of red spice.

I tell Siripan my grandfather fled Austria,
a famine, and the Great War. He mined
Pennsylvania coal, drifted from camp to camp,
met the woman washing long underwear
in a Johnstown boarding house. Later,
he slogged like a refugee for years,
fixing railroad tracks for American Zinc.

They traveled far to find their wives, she says
into my eyes. Our kiss feels like an ocean,
its waves breaking on opposite shores.

Between Daylight and Twilight

At 5 pm, Siripan looks at me
pretending not to look at her across
the wide English Department office.
The Day Director's gone and I can stop
blindly scanning the phonetics text.
With one side-glance, I know
she knows it's time for lessons in Thai.
She stands by my desk, holding vocabulary
on a sheet. My hand takes the page;
my other hand touches the delicate curve
of her calf, smooth as the rising
tone of the word *beautiful* in Thai.

We put the desk between us
in case a student pushes through
the swinging door of the department.
I learn phrases for *heaven,*
hell, nirvana as I reach down
and clasp her out-stretched ankles
under the desk and rest them
on my knees. We gaze into our mutual
smiles as the light pales to the milky
gray before twilight. With my feet I hook
her chair legs, pull her toward me,
bellies pressed into the desk between us.
We lock hands in clasping rapture

until the Twilight Director drifts in.
With our hands now empty
of each other, we *wai* him deeply
and Siripan slips on her shoes.

Dancing the Ramwong with Siripan

Her hands are bird's wings
dipping and hovering, fingers fanning out
feathery and quick.

She whirls, half sashay, half prance
like a starling on parade.

The "Thai waltz," teachers tell me,
and urge me to follow
Siripan's lead. My hands flutter
in imitation of flight, and drop like stones
when the music stops.

She's graceful, like the dance itself,
a formal stylized courting, spinning
through all the positions that turn
a man and woman into blossoms.

The science teachers watch us.
The math guy, Professor Geng,
calls me "Mr. Communist"
because my students wrote about
"poor teaching" in the school paper.
He snickers, asks loud enough
what Siripan sees in me.

As the band finishes, we sneak
out of the gym, and my fingers
weigh down her fluttering
bird-wing hands to my thighs.

Night Club

Black lights and strobes bathe the band
in flashes of darkness. The triangle guitars
and Day-Glo yellow drums scatter gleams
through the saccharine chords of "Feelings."
Siripan's old *farang* friend, between her
and me at the little table, gesticulates, pleads,
his back to me. Siripan gazes into her glass
of Singha beer. I can't follow his Thai
but *love you* jumps out like a minor chord
amidst the band's romantic dirge.

Chris, the "crazy *farang*" teacher at Bangkhen
three years before me, stormed the college.
Together he and Siripan taught Hemingway,
recited "Our Nada who art in Nada."
They put on Shakespeare plays.
The junior class production, abridged
English and makeshift stagecraft,
brought the Dean to see swordfights
and Antony sway the gullible crowd
(three ebullient students by the footlights),
yelling, *Go G. I., go get bad Brutus, kill.*
Caesar wore a pakama cloth for a toga
and a painted cardboard crown.
Now Chris puts on a show and Siripan
listens. He'll come back, marry her.

Shut out by their past, the language
and the dinky black table, I float
like the suspended disco ball
reflecting their bright intensity
in hundreds of mirrored fragments of rage,
helpless. Should I act like Hemingway,
grab his shoulder, punch his face,
and lose her forever? Roiling with feelings
should I sit silent, and lose her forever?
They once did *Hamlet*: a student stuttered,

"To be" and another echoed, "or not
to be." Chris had them join and finish
the speech together, prompting each other:
two choices, two Hamlets, no action.
Siripan looks up into his eyes: *I don't
love you.* And my *farang* hands
loosen on the throat of my beer.

November Full Moon

It's *Loy Krathong*, the night lovers float lit candle-boats
on waves, wish for luck from water spirits.
We two couples walk to the river. Yingna curses Harry
in bar-girl Thai I can't follow. Siripan drops my hand,
runs ahead of us into the shadows between streetlights.
Your girlfriend doesn't want to hear that shit, Harry says.
I chase Siripan down the narrow street under high walls
topped with jagged glass, glinting green in the moonlight.
When I touch her shoulder, Siripan's crying:
She said she'll sleep with every man on Patpong.
Sweat seeps into my shirt like ignorance.
I'm always insulting her with the best intentions.
I sit on the curb. She hails a cab, then waves it off.
Yingna followed Harry home one night and stayed.
She's pregnant. He won't marry her. Siripan gazes
down the road where a blue neon light flickers.

We find them again by the Chao Phraya River.
The rainy season over, China winds blow into Bangkok.
At the water's edge, Siripan calms Yingna.
Their silhouettes sway against the dark waves:
Siripan's Western pants and Yingna's peasant sarong
together in this city of walls. My palms cradle
a bamboo boat strung with jasmine,
sheltering a small yellow candle. We drift apart
into the privacy the night provides every few paces.
Her arm around Harry, Yingna shouts, *Ours is still lit!*
Some boats crowd together. Some spin
and float back to shore. Most flames die at ten yards.
Siripan and I squat on the muddy bank. My hissing match
whispers to the night air, and kisses the candle-wick
with fire. We push our boat into the current,
give the flame to the wind and waves.

With Yingna at the Hotel Opera Coffee Shop

She says her father sold her, 10,000 baht,
to a Bangkok bar. She says she accepts
her karma: to be poor and lovely,
proud of her skin, orange-cream,
smooth as Burmese women.

The life's never boring, she says
when Harry chooses her, 17 years old,
the only girl in the black-lit gallery
not watching Thai soaps,
but staring straight into the peep-hole's
glass swirl, a dark yin-yang.

He says her energy attracts him,
unpredictable as the rainy season sky.
Mornings, tourists' eyes follow her
tight jeans sashaying in the wall mirrors
of the Hotel Opera coffee shop. Smiling
at all of them, she slides her lithe,
compact shoulders and Coke bottle hips
against Harry in the booth, tells us secrets:

another bar-girl jumped on her belly
to jolt loose the child growing in her womb.
She says most girls wash down Valiums
with cold tea each night to make love
with the Australians, Americans,
Japanese, men from all over the planet.

Harry says she squats in the tub after sex,
squeezes out his semen. She leaves Thailand
with a German tourist, hides her bruises
from Harry returning three months later.
Once, she tries to slash her wrists
in front of him. He stops her. She hugs him,
loves him, as a drowning person still loves
the life-preserver that won't float,
for the pure comfort of the gesture.

It's the same way she describes the clouds
skimming the hilltops above her home village
in the Cold Season, or the warmth of rice

steaming on her mother's brazier,
assuring us she'll go back there some day.

Years later, Harry hears she entered
Khanita's shelter, then worked construction
shunting baskets of wet cement.

Temple of the Golden Buddha

Kwaam helps us take a coin to press
a foil-thin sheet of gold leaf
onto Buddha's peaceful cheekbones.
Among pungent incense, I rub off
a flaked shimmer just above the corner
of his smile, the gold brilliant
as the pineapple stacked cross-wise
like sliced sunshine on the vendor's cart.

Guarding the temple doors,
cement demons glitter
with broken porcelain from the holds
of Chinese ships, a rainbow of red,
purple, and green shards.
They place the demons to keep us in,
not out, but we don't listen.

Re-joining the fanged images
of ravaging desire, we enter the street,
and its raw beauty. Harry checks his wallet,
his dollars, his condoms.

Under a zenith sun he tramples
his shadow with his feet
seeking all joys but wisdom
among the metal-grated storefronts,
the butcher-shop, fortune-teller,
apothecary, serving the bodily
chakras of the city.

In the Thermae Bar, Yingna waits
for his purple Ray-bans, red,
sun-burned nose, and green silk shirt.
He's one of many, but tonight
she's his for most of the evening,
and longer, if he pays more
than the Australian she's with today.

Kwaam and I walk away
on hot cement, but Harry rides
a sampan, skimming canals
lined with shanties, a bouquet

of hibiscus, jasmine, orchids
in his lap, the purple blooms
more beautiful as the petals curl up
in the heat, precious as porcelain
on broken-off stems.

The Night House

After finals in phonetics class,
students disperse, fleeing
the white-tiered school building
above the lotus pond. Our questions
are a trap they've escaped.
Teaching English, we plant oaks
among the brilliant palms.
On weekends and mornings
before school, their phonemes,
morphemes are clicked and spat
at buffalos pulling the plow. Mud
sucks at their feet, pronouncing
its language of hold, release,
slosh, gush. The mud speaks
the old Thai of their fathers. Voices
in the flooded paddies at night
wrap their insect, frog, and snake
tongues around the little house
where the grandfather waits
to scare away wild boars.
The rice seedlings' thick green hair
bursts over mud dykes, enough shoots
in one square to transplant into 20
other paddies with rows of stalks.

Sonjay writes an English paper
about sleeping in the night house
with his *big father*, 87 years old,
who speaks Folktale with the phonetics
of ghosts, puffs of air, mysterious
fricatives. *A mother brings her son rice
in a too small basket. In anger
he kills her. But the magic basket
keeps replenishing the rice
so he has as much as the fields
will yield in time. He prays to Buddha
who tells him in the words of sutras
to build a temple to the lost
mother. She haunts the night houses
until dawn, and needs to rest.* Siripan
looks at me. The students have run off,

and we haunt the empty classrooms.
Sonjay's paper lies on my desk.
How can I grade its agreement
or tense? I want to hear the mother's
voice, her spirit calling like the frogs
in the paddies. Is that her, that magic
mother who speaks the language of rain,
husks, and the night house? Siripan
and I walk out into the evening
traffic where the students disappeared.
She smiles, and shakes her head.
We walk off in opposite directions
as palm leaves whisper in the wind.

Good-bye Party

*Thai people believe we all have a "khwan," a guiding spirit
that watches over us and keeps us whole.*
Kukrit Pramoj

We cook burgers on my bucket grill.
Baupit asks me about Elvis. *The king,*
I say. They've seen him in *Blue Hawaii,*
Viva Las Vegas, Girls, Girls, Girls!
in up-country towns. They are tongue-tied
in English class, but sing, *Don't be cruel,*
hound-dog, love me tender. We play baseball
in a nearby park, a chipped wooden bat
a frayed softball. I pitch to Em-on
in blue jeans. The shortstop catches
her fly ball. She's out, but runs to first
anyway. *I hit,* she says, *I stay.*

Evening on my deck, students hum
an ancient Thai song. Cymbals clang
low. One taps a drum; they sit around me
faces lit by flickering candles. Enthralled,
I glance at the moon plunging into pale clouds.
I'm ringed by their watchful eyes;
my class for two years, this is their way
to say goodbye. Em-on, now in Thai silk,
dances around me singing a prayer to Buddha
to keep my khwan from straying.

Her arms sweep candle-perfumed air;
her curved fingers unfold like fans
from her wrists. Circling me in the circle
of her classmates, she teaches me the grammar
of the spirit, the way candle smoke strays
up beyond her twirling hands into the sky
while her hips sway in a silk sarong
and her smile stays serene, unmoving.

Up-Country
๒

From the Window

The train pulls from Bangkok station,
away from Siripan, from the closed
school and into a myth of rice fields.
What's older, the farmer plowing
a glass sea, or the idea
of motion, wheels and wind?

A small blue comma, the man's body,
hunches over the plow in the distance,
moves in half-steps behind
the buffalo. The train car lurches
forward, jerking through humid air.
Above the tiny farmer,
a mountainous, white cloud rises.

A canal, 1,000 years deep, gleams
between the tracks and paddies, white
as steam, bright as steel, narrow as rain.

Like a Stone Under Water

On a sagging spit, a roasting pig turns,
drips hissing, hot grease on coals.
Its bristly jowls droop sadly, then lift
to a skewered smile as its chin rotates skyward,
its tiny eyes slitted. How can it bear
that massed meaty flesh on such small legs?

Saffron-robed monks sit on a shaded platform,
shaved, serene, waiting for Van Childress
to welcome them. Soldiers ring the field,
rifles at ease in sweat-darkened jungle fatigues.
The province mayor, village headmen
claim first-row seats. Dark-suited, dark-haired
businessmen gleam like their black Audis
parked in red dust near an ancient Banyon.

Childress stands up, sandy hair rimming
his bald head, strangely frail for a man
who crossed the Cambodian border,
braved land mines, Khmer Rouge patrols
to glimpse Angkor Wat. He's my friend
from too many nights in bars, from rambling
conversations that last till dawn.
In the jungle above the village,
he excavated a Khmer mausoleum's toppled
stones, freed them from roots and vines.
Now the monks bless the resurrected pillars,
chant rhythmic Sanskrit to dead warlords,
coaxing their spirits into the ground.

***

At sundown, I tour the fair. Arc lights
boom with moths, carve fluorescent day
from black night. A mantis prays
in shadows. Chuay's wide, gap-toothed smile,
follows me. In tattered shorts, dusty coxcomb
of tufted hair, he shuffles on blistered feet.
Is he the village crazy man, drawn
to my pidgin Thai, blue jeans, and silk shirt

with its painted jungle of wild colors?
Give wis-a-key, please. I buy him rot gut.
He laughs when I laugh, drinks
when I drink: *You, GI, have cigarette?*

He pushes me toward hot lights
and mini-skirted women bussed from Korat.
The girls jerk their arms like moody puppets
in a cloud of glare to the bop, bop beat
of "Won't You Be True?" A girl lurches
close, kisses my earlobe: *I love you,*
20 baht. My hands grip her shoulders,
steadying her, and me, before she recedes
under rainbow lights. Behind the stage,
Chuay sways his hips and howls.

***

Haunoman, the white demon monkey
in the *Ramakien* opera, dances under dream
lamps, their papery globes like pale moons.
He chases Princess Lakshmi, but she hides
in a paper mache thundercloud. Kids
kickbox in a ring, their bloody foreheads
crowned with flowers. Chuay dozes beside me.
A stranger tugs me out of a drunken dream,
leads me outside the fair and disappears.
Under trees, my friend Childress sprawls
on the ground. Blood seeps from his temple.
The Khmer bastard, he moans. *Hit me*
with a chair. I chased him and fell.
My rubbery arms can't lift him. I yell
for help, run toward the fair's glow.

The air fills with spirits. A ghost
taps my shoulder, just an apple
someone threw. A man shouts, *Farang!*
A shadow grabs my shirt. Fingers grip
my hair. My wild fear imagines
scimitar claws, white fangs, the fierce
demi-gods in the opera. *Hey you,*
GI? Chuay? The dark shade tackles me,

his forearm on my throat, choking,
pressing his body against me. A hand clutches
my groin. I become beating fists, flailing
at dark bones, hot breath, grasping nails.

I break free, run. The jungle howls:
crickets *om*, mosquitoes screech, frogs
sing their guttural come-cries. I hide
in brush. A mashing, ticking, grating
sound surrounds me, low, distinct,
growing out of a layered silence,
like the whole world feeding on itself.
In darkness above me, cages hang from limbs:
silkworms munching mulberry leaves.

***

Back at the fair, I rub my cut knuckles
in dewy grass, wipe at a red paw-print
on my pants. The village sleeps. The fair
grinds on like its drawn-out dream
or nightmare, a mad one-night museum
of human fate. Above trampled grass,
a silver fountain rises, beaded
with light. Up close, it's a tree
of arcing steel wires. Paper leaves
festoon its gleaming limbs.

A pudgy man smiles: *Take number,*
ten baht. He palms my crumpled money,
stamped with the king's image. I pick a leaf
from the picked-over tree. He unhooks
an ivory Buddha on a thread of string,
loops it around my neck. *You luck best.*
The Buddha hangs on my chest,
smooth as a stone that's been sunk
in flowing water for 25 centuries.
I sit on the grass, back against a tree,
dozing, bruised, adrift in a starry sea.

***

Towards morning, I find Childress.
He sits in his bungalow on a bamboo mat,
faint kerosene light. Bloody gauze
slips off a cherry-bomb bruise
on his bald head. *When I left Fresno*
I had long hair. I built their temple,
and I'm still a farang. He grins,
showing cigarette-stained teeth, says
he threw the Khmer's chairs into a pond
because he charged too much
for Pepsi. *A few more days here,*
then I'm gone. In the gold light, my hands
shine white as the demon monkey
in the *Ramakien.* Far off, a temple bell
gongs the end of night as the village
glimmers in the first dawn.
I touch the Buddha. I sleep with it on.

J Fail the "Real Thai" Test

The backyard table is strewn
with bowls of hairy red rambutans,
strips of grilled steak, onions,
peppers, and glass flasks
of Mekong Whiskey.

Chueng, with a wizened face
and neck mole sprouting a tuft
of long hairs, yells, *For you, Professor!*
Thank you, I say, and he hands me
a bulging banana leaf wrapped around
dripping beef and vegetables.

I should notice all their faces lit
with drunk glee, the flourish, the mock
formality of his bow
as he offers it in both hands.

My tongue is a hot coal. Fire
spreads to my gums, the walls
of my mouth, down my throat. Inside
the leaf, a cornucopia-shaped pepper
spills seeds and juice. *Is good?*

He wants me to smile, jump up,
fan my mouth with a frantic hand,
yell for water, a good sport.
But I sit still, and angrily
turn away in a cavernous silence.

In the Hot Season

On wide, brown water, a boy floats
on waves dimpling in the sun.
The river's starved of rain. Tree roots
show through like gray ribs
near the banks. From the bridge,
I watch his silver canoe, a packing tin
emptied of bamboo shoots. Hand-paddling
into the slow drift of the current,
he lies back, face to the sky.

He wears only blue shorts,
his school uniform. His cotton shirt
is a white flag draped over the side, signaling
his surrender to a day without desire.
His eight-fold path lies across
low water cradled by gnarled hills.
In the lazy sway of the box,
his back rests against the cool river,
the hot tin gunwales gleaming.

As the rumbling, spattering caravan
of trucks, buses and *tuk-tuks* pass
over him on the bridge on their raucous
way to Bangkok, the Angel City,
he floats diamond-bright and solitary
in the middle of the sweltering town.
Halfway from either bank, he finds
the bright center of the afternoon.

Barubador Temple

Stacked higher than I can reach,
stairs cut a groove into massive stones.
The walls writhe with human sutras
of rock cut in relief. One man's
money bags weigh him down,
a couple intertwines in sex, a farmer
plows. They pursue their karma
step by higher step, where students study
in schools, temples, before images
of Buddha, each person intent,
wounded with erosion and wedded
to the wall that forms them.

Near the top, the sky opens
to 360 degrees of blue above
the green tangle of jungle.
Monk statues sit on stone pedestals,
meditate in serene lotus positions
in the darkness of checkered stone bells
imprisoning them. Light enters
through the holes. They are trapped,
incarcerated by their carnal pasts.

It's cooler in wind and sun. Insects,
bus exhaust, creeper vines
ensnaring noble fig trees, lotus stars
bursting on the ponds like silent
fireworks all lie below. Am I free
of anything, panting from the climb?
My keys jingle in my pocket.
My wallet hangs in a pouch
from my neck, pressed on my heart.
My clothes sag, darkened by sweat.

I breathe air, sky, a firmament
where clouds meet the dust of busses,
taxis, groups of world travelers
aching for sunsets and exotic
fruit salads. If I wasn't so in love
with stones, I could be the one
monk statue sitting free, nothing but air
and light around me at the temple's
apex. I stand next to him, undo
my sandals, and press my feet
on the stone, the temple, the hill.

Up-country

Cymbals and tambourines clang. Students sing
on the up-country bus to Ampon's house
in his small village near the Gulf of Siam.
Next day, he'll show us his secret beach.
Outside the bus, night jungle looms
in shadows of headlights. Above the dash,
white jasmine leis dangle and sway
like us, as we clap and shout songs
to keep the groggy bus driver awake.

That night, we triple up under mosquito nets.
At dawn his mother cooks us eggs and rice cakes.
Ampon leads us between razor-leaf plants
under a green sky of trees. *Kaa, kaa,* blue wings
flit adroitly away. *A jungle bird,* Ampon says.
It speaks Thai, "What price, how much?"
He finds his beach: forest, white sand,
humpbacked waves. We body surf in loincloths.
Without me, they would have gone in naked.

At noon Ampon swims far out, waving
for us to follow. He crests in high frothy surf,
his head dwindling among flashes of light.
He sinks and we wait as the angry curl
flattens on the sand, hissing, empty.
We spread out, wade into shoving swirls.
Undertow sucks at our knees. *Ampon!*
Far down the beach, a limp body rolls,
shoved by breakers, limbs flinging like a doll's.

Jaloon lifts Ampon's shoulders from the water,
cradles his sand-flecked forehead in his lap.
Why did he go out so far? he asks the sky.
Brine oozes from Ampon's lips. Shit drains out.
We clean him with a pakama cloth, weeping
over his sunken cheeks, his eyes like quartz.
We kneel, silent. The waves crash into us.
A student rocks on his haunches, moaning,
What will we say to his father and mother?

We lift his stiffening body in a sling
like ants scurrying around a larval egg.
The bluish birds call, *Kaa, kaa.*
Word spreads through the palms, mangoes
and village streets. His father descends stairs
under his house, walks out into the light,
watching me. My skin never feels so white.
In the house, his mother wails, prepares the body.
I look at the floor: *Ampon was a good student.*

By evening friends bring food. Monks chant.
They raise the coffin on a high stack of wood.
The bonfire flames reach for Ampon
in the box, the horror eases, his face put to rest,
cleansed. It's the right thing, to burn him
before the sun rises again. The flames crackle,
engulf the box like the waves that pulled
him under. We sigh in droning ripples,
our arms around each other. It's finished.

The coffin falls open around Ampon's blackened
body. Sparks leap. A cry. Some turn away
as his skin bubbles, hisses, and the skull glows.
I move toward the fire, wanting to hold
his charred flesh in the saffron flames. His spirit
escapes with sparks up into stars. In this country,
they don't build the coffin to hold together.
Next morning, Ampon's nothing but ashes,
gray and white, lighter than wind.

The Dream of Culture
๓

The Day after the Coup

A green wall of jungle blazes outside
the window of the English Department room.
The professors wear their uniforms today,
creased and rumpled from being folded in trunks.
In stifling heat, we're made to stand at attention
like laurel leaves shrunk stiff in a cold snap.
Stocky soldiers in camouflage fatigues
weave between us. The sergeant grunts sharp
questions. Like a schoolmaster, he jabs at papers
with the grooved steel tip of his bayonet.

Later, we take chicken and *som tam* salad,
to three teachers in jail. Kwaam sits
cross-legged on cement in striped
prison shorts, his shirt draped over his neck
like a towel. Purple bruises shine
through the sweat on his chest.
We pass packets of yellow papaya
between the bars. His house burned down
last night. *Professor,* he whispers to me,
how do you like our Thai prisons?

Professor Som's still missing. *I hope he stays
in the mountains,* Suthep says. It's night.
We talk on his porch as frogs whistle
love calls in the canals. He's my boss, the newly
appointed dean. Moths fly into the candlelight
and fall, splashing, in a wide water pan
he set on the table to catch them. Turned low,
his police radio murmurs about students barricaded
in a Bangkok university, fighting tanks.

Communist dogs, he growls. *They have guns
in their rooms, make trouble for everyone.*
I ask what will happen. He shrugs.
The soldiers will kill them. I take the pan
and pour the moths onto the ground,
set it back on the table again. One flops over,
legs grasping at air. Others lie drowned
on the grass. Suthep says good night,
pinches out the flame with his thumb.

Kukrit

for Kukrit Pramoj (1911-1995)

Kukrit was Prime Minister twice,
once in a Hollywood movie, *The Ugly
American*, and once for real.
What did he think, putting on the mask
of a repressive Thai aristocrat,
corruption oozing from his half-smile?
*I'd make my mother-in-law chief
of police if she were qualified.*
He waves a cigarette, blows smoke
up toward the icy light of chandeliers.
When Communist revolutionaries clamor
outside his door, the American ambassador
can't believe the serene smile
on his full-moon face: *If my head
must end up on a spike in the public
square, I want it to be smiling.*

As he plays at being overthrown,
does he dream that later he'll be deposed
for real, this time by the right? He leads
the Social Action Party against the National
Party. His opponent, a former general,
calls him gay. *Send your wife to my house,
and we'll see,* Kukrit replies. He bribes
MPs to give a "seed and feed" credit card
to farmers. A right wing song mocks:
*Farmers won't be thinking. They'll use
the cards for whiskey drinking.* Soon US troops
leave Thailand. He goes to China like Nixon,
meets with Mao, bargains for protection
from battle-hardened Vietnamese troops
raiding Thai villages on the border.

After 14 months, nervous generals
arrest him, set up an autocrat like the one
he played in the movie a decade before.
Students hang in public parks, their bodies
spit on, stomped on.

His Royal Majesty King Bhumibol Visits an Up-country Town

Are you the water or the wave?
Roman proverb

For days, workers assemble a walkway
with wooden rails. A two-by-four roof
covered by thatch, zigzags the grass field.
For days people arrive by bus, train,
and buffalo cart to camp outside the fair grounds
ringed with soldiers in kakhis and carbine rifles.

For days, villagers beg busy lieutenants
to lay their silk and cotton pakama cloths,
pillow cases, head scarves on the path
he will walk, a sacred keepsake
sanctified by the low shoe sole
of the highest person in the kingdom.

They line the path fifty strong in sun and heat:
rice farmers, clerks, teachers, trishaw drivers,
sellers from the closed market, ditch-diggers,
truck drivers. They pass rose petals
for those at the railing to scatter beneath his feet.

Now the far edge of the field blooms
with waving arms. Cheers crescendo, bodies
sway together until soldiers with machine guns
wade the human sea. Their hands press down
as if paddling water and the crowd falls
to their knees, a human tsunami rolling toward us.

The roar peaks. He appears, his frail thin frame
in a white suit coat, the child-like, solemn face,
on the money, in theaters, portraits
in every office and school room. On the path,
he turns, waves, his glinting glasses
hide his eyes. Smiling, he surveys a field
of prostrate bodies like a calmed ocean.

Afterwards, the sea rises. Cheers fade.
People surge to and fro. Stumbling forward
like a happy drunk, a man lifts his pakama
in the air never to be worn again, but tucked

secretly into a drawer. An old woman cradles
a handful of rose petals she picked
out of the mud, inhales their sweet perfume.

A few slip from her fingers and flutter
like red butterflies to the ground.
She kneels, gathers them from the trampled
grass and passing feet. Sunlight slants
over the field, a rainy season storm brewing.
People clutch their sacred souvenirs, stagger
into the city like surf sinking into sand.

Traffic Circle

Movie billboards blot out a six-story building.
This Week: a bare-chested man kung-fu kicks
against a flaming yellow background, leaps over
tiny scampering armies while cities burn.
Coming Soon: a prisoner, handcuffed in blue rags,
towers sadly over the sidewalk. In painted insets
a judge ponders scales; a woman fingers a gun.

Below, where the scaffold-poles rise from grass,
families live. A mother shifts a steaming pot
on a charcoal brazier. Her boy chases chickens.
Their laundry hangs under the burning cities
and the huge feet of the prisoner.

The Teak House

Kukrit's teak house floats on stilts
above white walls topped with jagged glass
around Bangkok mansions. Its high-peaked
sloped roofs glide above Betel Tree Lane
and the city smog. On windy days,
the house sings wood on wood
through the creaking teak pegs
holding the five sections together.

The teak house sings with mandolins,
bong drums, cymbals as Kukrit dances
surrounded by students. His puffy silk sleeves
flap around him, the gold *khon* mask
reflecting klieg lights of Thai TV. His hands
whirl like kites in the winds of his emotions.

Mornings, he rises from the desk
where he revised Thailand's constitution,
and wrote his novels: *Red Bamboo,*
Four Reigns, Many Lives. His three dogs pant
and bark for his attention. Their teeth have gouged
the wooden legs of the table and chairs.

He keeps 2,000 fish, knows the names for each:
Haunoman, the white angel fish, Thanom
and Sarit, red and black anglers
named for generals who opposed him,
and Loi and Sem, goldfish he named after
a thief and a monk in his stories.
He feeds them, smiling, then meditates
in a room filled with Buddhas, serene,
laughing, crouching, reclining.

He recites a favorite sutra, walking
down the stairs by the two pear-shaped vases
Mao gave him in China, and the portraits
of his royal grandparents gazing from a palace
chamber decked with saffron curtains.

In the garden he walks among bonsai pines
and the trained palm trees dwarfed
in small pots, but the wind sings through
the huge betel trees ringing the yard,
whispering memories. He thinks of Oxford,
his years travelling three continents.

He could have lived in any city of the world.
Coming home from 10 years abroad,
he writes: *For days on the train, I watch
my country go by — paddies, palms, canals,
dirt roads, the steep, orange-tiled
temple roofs — and I don't get tired of it.*

Thai-ness

Thai-ness: "a sublime, responsible enjoyment of life."

In Kukrit's novel of the old Monarchy,
Lady Phloi lives through four Thai kings.
In the queen's chamber, she learns Thai-ness
with the young palace girls, patiently
carving betel nuts into the faces of princes.

In the sacred tonsure ceremony at 11 years old
monks cut her childhood topknot
with a golden knife, chanting: *Dear Khwan*
do not stray in the waters and caves
of the forest, come and stay in this child's body.

From a golden spoon Phloi eats egg
and coconut milk three times
as the monks bang a gong, shout *Ho*
like an earthquake, to inform the gods
she's learned Thai-ness. She prays
to the Triple Gem: the Buddha,
his Teachings, and the Monks.

Four kings burn to glorious ash.
Four queens weep as Phloi sits with the women
learns Thai-ness, keeping calm, chewing
betel nut, that stains her lips and teeth
crimson, then spits the red juice.

Phloi Says Good-bye to Her Favorite Trees before Leaving for the Palace

Goodbye wide-crowned cork tree.
I made pretend curry for the King
under your wide branches. I helped mother
gather your wide flowers, curled
like a *farang* woman's hair. We soaked them
in hot honey, mixed in Muang Song tobacco,
pressed the mulch and dried it in the sun.
Mother cut the parched leaves in ovals
and rolled them into father's favorite cigars.

Good-bye night-flowering jasmine,
aromatic as the temple incense
and the flowers we take to Madame Teacher.
Mother crushed your red-stemmed blooms
in the *som tam* bowl and poured
the scarlet juice into the trough
to dye her lovely blouses.

Good-bye Rubiaceae tree. Thank you
for letting me pick your sweet
white star blossoms. Mother wove them
into ribbons and garlands. They fluttered
in the wind from my topknot of black hair.

Thank you and good-bye great mango tree,
best-tasting fruit in all of father's province.
Your saffron slices lay glistening
like a shining temple roof
on the sweet square of sticky rice.

Banyon by the sala, good-bye.
You are a forest all your own,
dropping roots from your branches
which become new trees, new lives, falling
farther and farther from the grandfather
in the center. How much you have grown
since when I climbed you
with my older brother as a child.
Good-bye, banyon of my family,
tree palace of my home.

The Land of Transit

Two Farangs

He's naked except for flip-flops
and frayed jeans cut-off
above mid-thigh and tight
around his bulging belly.

*Look, at that farang strutting
down the sidewalk,* I think,
sweaty, hairy chest and shock
of frizzed, blond hair bright
in sunlight. Ragged pants,
no shirt, that beard.

I'm about to cross the street
to warn him we Thais
find big white bodies unsettling
as ghosts, until I glimpse
my pale reflection in a store
window, my round *farang* eyes
staring back at me in wonder.

Suang U's Letters from Thailand

I walked away in pre-dawn light from Po Leng,
through fields we farmed for years.
I remembered the scrawl I left for you
on the kitchen table: "Forgive me, mother."
On a freighter big as our village and packed
with immigrants, I sailed from China
to Thailand. Writing this letter to you
on the boat, I felt a hand on my shoulder.
A Chinese importer praised my fine calligraphy,
adopted me as his son, promised a job.

In Shanghai, a Communist official
picks up Suang U's letter, runs his finger
over the Thai stamp Suang U glued
to the envelope, slips the steel blade
of a letter-opener under the flap.

Mosquitoes swarmed our boat in Bangkok harbor.
My new father took me by trishaw
through shop-lined streets bursting with bolts
of silk, tree-lined canals, and fire leaping from woks.
The Chinese driver said I must leave the old
dreams behind. A fine, fat yellow sun, mother,
a great many fruit trees, what do they do
with so many coconuts and pineapples?

In Shanghai, the official opens another
letter. He's hooked on Suang U's story
and the Chinese money folded neatly
inside the paper. He slips the letter
into his drawer with the others.

I sat close to my boss' daughter on the grass,
teaching her to read from a romance novel
about Old China. Like the heroine in the story,
she left her pearls for me between
the pages. I called her "the face of the moon."
Why don't you answer me, mother?
I want you to see my new bride.

In Shanghai the official, now a censor
for the Party, raises an eyebrow and smiles
when he sees the Thai king on the stamp.
He fondles the long letters, takes them home
to read in the evening after dinner
with his tea. Just like a novel, he chortles
to himself. Far better than bland news
or stale propaganda about Mao.

Ten years now, I have my own import store.
I sit under my shelves stocked with tea pots,
teak furniture, hand-woven silk. Bright neon glows
above my metal grate at night. Lazy Thais jeer,
call me "foreigner" and "chink face." They're drunks,
gamblers, fighters. My years feel empty
as a leaking rice sack. My daughter shamed me,
married the son of a Thai street vendor, her pushcart
filled with gelatinous squares of rose and green,
her fingers sticky with coconut, her toothless smile.

Letter after letter, the official Chinese censor
reads about bright skies, gold chedis reaching
to the heavens and markets filled with spices,
so many strange foods: *rambutan, jackfruit,*
durian, not listed in his Chinese dictionary.

Electric wires smoked and sparked. Silk, red and gold,
grew wings of flame. Later I wandered through
the collapsed shop, sunk in ashes. My son
had no room for me. My Thai son-in-law smiled,
handed me a lotus, an orchid, took me in.

In Bangkok, a Thai customs official opens
a trunk. Hundreds of letters, 22 years worth,
lie scattered among the clothes. *They're mine,*
the official censor yells. He has defected,
wants asylum in the land of plenty. In a jail cell,
he tells the police the story of the letters.

In Po Leng, Suang U's mother walks by Dazibou,
and the children painting angry red slogans,
condemning the old ways of capitalism.
She's too poor to matter, and passes away
with the only note from her son
she ever received, *Forgive me, mother,*
clutched in her hand.

Night Train

In the sleeper's dim light,
the wheels bang the rails
da-dig-a-da-dik all night
echoing his name two hours
out of Nakhon Ratchasima:
time to think if I ever got straight
with him. The moon in the wavy glass
of rice paddies wobbles
and stretches in all directions
pliable as memory, . . .

but the hard disc in the sky faces me,
unshakable as the glance
of the American Consul outside
my classroom: *Your father's dead.*
The dark palms, earthen dikes,
the paddies' black sheen
speed by under the face
etched by craters, mountain shadows,
and the glistening sands of the Sea
of Serenity, the Ocean of Storms.

The Land of Transit

The country within
every country is the land of transit,
Einstein's world
at a fraction of light-speed
in motion in the air
on wheels, on rails, in lobbies,
jail cells, immunity rooms,
the land beyond
jobs, home, sequestered
under TVs hung in airport bars
people slouched in chairs,
the vinyl limbo of transit.

In the land of transit, a boulder falls
toward our bus on the road
to Lake Toba, misses us
by yards at a hairpin turn, falls
in the slow-motion time of a thousand
foot drop, and shatters the river.

In the land beyond time
and being in time, three Brit teens
on a bus to Bali buy drugs
in Jakarta, offer me a hit
in a roadside restroom.
We're high in the land of transit,
our only job to hurry,
weighed down, queued up,
on dusty linoleum by the closed
ticket booth that opens
in three hours.

In Delhi, time becomes elastic,
playful. A Sikh clerk takes his sweet
time processing my visa. I fidget:
My plane to Bangkok is leaving!
Americans don't know how to wait.
He smiles, stacks the papers,
arranges the pens, settles
in his chair, teaching me to see
the drab flag on the wall
the ceiling fan, the woman nursing a child

behind me. *Don't worry*, he says,
in India, minutes are longer.

The land of transit is not on time,
but in time, like a current
that carries me at its speed, transparent,
no bottom to its clear stream
as I pass soldiers with rifles,
a push-cart of Thumbs Up Cola,
a woman drinking from her hand
at the public fountain, the seller
displaying hundreds of rings. Children
in rags outside Calcutta station,
tug at my shirt and hold out empty
hands, as if offering me time.
My coins sink into their palms
down into a bottomless streambed
and the current carries them away.

The country within all
countries (this one in Myanmar),
confiscates my 200 US dollars,
pushes me up against a wall,
spread eagle, then into a detention
cell. Bare bars, cement floor,
the rusty drain hole in the center
is the only other way out.
It's the black space
where time is taken away.

A Mandalay dawn, five AM
airport tarmac. A mosque stands
far away, dark and intricate
against infinite blue light embering
above low hills. We lug
our separate ages with weary steps
toward a woman in a sari.
She sits on a plaid suitcase
beside a stairway on wheels
that waits for the late plane. I look up
between the metal railings beyond
the raised platform, out into the middle
of nowhere, the blue land of transit.

Walking the Beach with Harry in Southern Thailand, Thinking of My Father

The sun rises above sparkling waves,
and a corridor of light leads to the Pacific
far beyond the Gulf of Siam. It sets now

in America. It's noon in Hawaii where my father
landed at Pearl Harbor in 1943. They shipped him
to "God-awful" Canal in time for the bloodiest

battles. *Nothing but mud, malaria,*
jungle rot, he told us kids. Maybe it's nine AM
there. Probably the trees have reclaimed

the air field where a pilot he grounded
pulled a .45 on him. Glazed eyes, battle
fatigue, the loss of a copilot to Japanese flak

made everyone his enemy. The white sand
blinds Harry and me in a palm-rimmed cove.
Fishing boats, black silhouettes dot the water,

smooth like the harbor at Efate where my father
saw the white outline of the Enterprise looming
over its 20-boat task force: *Gosh it was beautiful.*

By the Hundred-Foot Reclining Buddha

Firefly
sizing up
Mt. Fuji
Issa

The red ant walks at my feet
on the sand swept so fine
that nothing grows.

Monks can't step on grass or roots
let alone this tiny saffron
creature an inch long.

Below the Buddha
reclining in front of me,
I am an inch-long *farang*.

The Buddha's knowing
smile, the ant's mandibles
articulate a delicate contrast:
Do I know everything,
or nothing? His huge toes

tower over me as my toes
tower over the ant.
The sunlight, hot on my head
glints off the Buddha

in smashed patches of gold.
The ant ascends
the pedestal to journey
across his hot stone robes.

Day of Making Merit

Silver full moon among palm leaves
follows us in procession
on the Day of Making Merit.
Three times around the temple walls,
monks lead us. The abbot recites
sutras until midnight, chanting
over cymbals. A cool March wind
polishes the stars, cuts through
the sala's open-air space
and the words of Thai sermons.
Both will last until dawn.
Cross-legged, listening, I catch
phrases: *Do not desire desire.*
I fall asleep, hunched over,
my forehead on the mat, imagining
Siripan next to me. I'm a bad audience
on the Day of Making Merit.

Up-country Dream

> *"You've paid for all your previous sins and karma.*
> *Go and be reborn in your chosen place. Take refuge in the Buddha."*
> Sem, the Monk in Kukrit's story

In the dream, I'm a *farang* as always
sitting in a deserted dirt-floor shop,
the King's picture above the brazier.

Grandma Blair in a blue sarong stirs
fried rice in a wok, her spatula clanging
in the hiss of oil and egg as she flips

the steaming rice. A motorcycle spatters
in the street. She shakes her head
at me, pours the hot mix onto a plate

and sets it at my place. The rider
on the motorcycle sits across from me,
takes off his helmet. Kukrit, the PM

in *The Ugly American*, that smiling face,
watches me. My hands tremble
with foreboding. I'll soon be arrested.

The rice on my plate turns to worms
roiling around my chopsticks.
Why aren't you eating? Kukrit asks.

I look toward the street. *Siripan's not here,*
he says. *She can't help you. Not when you spit
in the well you drink from. You farangs*

*have lice in your hair, dreaming
that you're royalty.* He grabs my topknot,
pushes my face into the worms.

Grandma, I take refuge in the Buddha, I yell.
My face in pillows, I hear the slow turning blades
of my ceiling fan: *farang, farang, farang.*

Vientiane

I'm 21, a hot zenith sun
gleams off orange roof tiles
like the first light of dawn
and the last light of dusk
on clouds. No shade, no dark.
What lies under my soles
is only dust, where Whitman
said we would find him waiting.

For an instant nothing
has shadow or doubt. The heat
on top of my head kindles
all things sentient and non-
sentient. For once, I'm not
a sundial, a clock, a timepiece,
not a watch that watches
what I am not, but what
I am, which is everything.

I swat a mosquito. My shadow
arm appears to strike myself.
A tree shadow spills
from the well of its own darkness
to one side like a word
for "tree," like a song of myself
out of tune, nostalgic, that instant

now in the past. At night, neon
shadows scatter across our table
in an up-country bar. A grizzled
expatriate US Marine squints
into his shot glass. His voice
glows with religious fervor:
*Vientiane, Laos, 1969: the best ass
and the best grass in the world.*

Planting Rice with Nipun, Ubol Province

My bare feet wading ankle-deep water,
I face a buffalo's tapered back flanks,
and the leathery black zero
of its anus. We work a glassy rice paddy
among hundreds of gleaming squares
checkering the flat valley. In the distance, the blue
mounded Petchabun mountains rise into Laos.

Don't push the plow down.

I guide the curved wood-tip through soft mud.
He clicks his tongue, tugs a rope
strung through the buffalo's spongy nose.
It turns at the dike and we slosh along,
shattering the sky below us.
Soon Nipun drapes my neck with a cloth,
gives me a green bundle of rice shoots.

Do three rows, like this.

He plants a shoot off his left foot,
one below his crotch, and one off his right.
I bend, thumb-jam the seedlings' roots
into cool viscous muck. The mud
holds them, tight as my ankles.

Don't raise your back. Sing with me.

Forced to grip new soil,
the green spears totter and wave.
We step, reach, stretch, swinging
our arms and singing
the planting song's tonal Thai words:

During the twelfth full moon,
canals overflow their banks.
All the rice farmers dance
under the village locust tree.

That night, we sip rice wine
around an open fire. Heat-lightning flashes
off the capes of horizon clouds.
Overhead, Orion, old silver warrior,
wields his starry shield and sword, forever locked
in battle with the bull. Nipun smiles.

For Thai farmers, it's a turtle
with a plow on its back. See?
The belt and the sword make a plow.

I nod and stretch my muddy feet to the fire,
my body stiff and sore from plunging
hundreds of roots into earth.

Back in Pittsburgh for My Father's Funeral

In O'Rourke's Bar and Grill, a mile
from where I grew up, I'm a *farang*. Jim, Rob,
Gerry, John greet me with hard handshakes,
booming my name into the loud music.

Sorry, about your dad.

I've known them since grade school,
and haven't seen them for years. We trade stories:
Bangkok heat from me, marriages, new jobs,
and children from them. But what I expect
to see throws me: not Singha quart bottles
but Iron City ponies on the table,

not sunshine on the wide Bangkok boulevards
and palm trees waving in glare, but overcast sky,
narrow streets hugging hillsides, my tires
drumming cobblestones between old steel rails.

So, how's "Thigh"-land? Jim asks with a wink.
It's okay. The American soldiers have left.

I picture Siripan's saffron face
at the faculty play. She's the princess
in the *Ramakien*, skin tinted with turmeric
and talcum powder. Flashes of her costume
ripple through my mind.

How's roofing? I ask John, his hands like sand paper.
Last week, he says they faked a drunken fight
in the middle of Oakland, a crowd watching,
then slipped away before the police arrived.

On TV, the Steeler quarterback throws
a long arcing ball caught by the receiver's
outstretched fingers. It's Monday night when I play
takraw with my students, leaping, kicking
a wicker ball over a net, no hands.
John and Rob have tennis night Thursdays.
They play touch football Sundays. They tease me
about soccer, kickboxing, and *takraw.*

*Those sports are like playing footsie
in eighth grade,* says Jim. *It's from the rice,*
Gerry chimes in, all-knowing, wise-ass:
Football is steak and sex. I smile.
Later I walk out in cold November drizzle.
In my father's Monte Carlo, my hands hold
the same wheel he held for years.

Driving the old streets I spot a blue bicycle
like the one I ride everyday in Ubol.
I want to follow it, as the rain thickens
into curtains between us, want to believe
its wavering silhouette will guide me home.

Making Sticky Rice on Edgerton Place

I pour the dry white grains into water.
Golden chaff rises to the surface.
Remembering the rice's bready smell,
the roots of my teeth stir, anticipating
its sticky sweetness. I ate it plain,
or wrapped in banana leaves and roasted
over coals, crunchy outside, a raisin hidden
in the center. I ate it with Siripan,
at Professor Kwaam's party.
In the cool season wind, I drove her home
on my bicycle. He came running
with a basket of sticky rice:
For later tonight. Now I stir the pan.
In the water, a curled brown thing wakes,
moves tiny antennae, legs hugging
a swelling rice grain. After 12,000 miles,
years in dry sacks, months on a shelf
at Kim Do Store, this creature revives
in the ricey water like a seed
opening, a memory: Siripan's smile
as she lifted her dress around her thighs
wading in the Mekong's moonlit waves.

About the Poet

Peter Blair's most recent book is *The Divine Salt* (2003) published by Autumn House Press. His earlier book, *Last Heat* (Word Works Press) won the Washington Prize in 1999. Born in Pittsburgh, he has worked in a psychiatric ward, a steel mill, and served three years in the Peace Corps in Thailand. Currently, he teaches at the University of North Carolina at Charlotte.

Design and Production

Cover and Text Design by Esther Harder
Cover Photos by Steven Harder
Poet Photo by Wade Bruton

Text set in Bell MT, designed in 1992 by Monotype Typography
Titles set in Kawoszeh, designed in 2008 by Grzegorz
    for openfontlibrary.org

Thai script set in Twlg Typist, designed in 2005
    by Theppitak Karoonboonyanan of Thai Linux Working Group

The Thai word "ฝรั่ง" used in this book is *Farang*, translated into
Thai characters. The Thai numerals representing Arabic numerals
1-4 are used on the section break pages.

Printed by BookMobile™ (www.bookmobile.com) of Minneapolis,
Minnesota, on Natural Finch Opaque Vellum, a certified Archival
Quality acid-free paper